An Unfaded

Meditations on Light and Silence

MARY BURTON

With Paintings by the Author

BURNS & OATES

First published in Great Britain in 1997 by
BURNS & OATES
Wellwood, North Farm Road,
Tunbridge Wells, Kent TN2 3DR

ISBN 0 86012 277 8

Typeset by Search Press Limited
Printed and bound in Spain by Elkar S. Coop. Bilbao 48012

A Word of Thanks

The author gratefully acknowledges the contributions of Patrick Casement, Alan Jones, Flor O'Callaghan, Michael Sadgrove and Colin Semper in discussions about this book. Special thanks go to Eugene Gendlin who wrote:

> Why *does* the infinity come through how the light plays on things? Please tell me any shred of understanding you have of why that is. I'm smiling. What a question to send you to answer!

This book is the result.

Thanks to Paul Burns who has enabled this book see the light of day, and to my teachers Charles Bartlett and Bob Kilvert who have encouraged me in the art of watercolour painting.

rustling wind in an autumn field of standing corn,
geese queueing up to cross a bridge,
willows in deep shadow in the river bed,
a flight of crows.[1]

Foreword

by Gerard W. Hughes, S.J.

After our death I imagine that God will probably ask most of us, "Why did you keep looking for me in the wrong places? I have been with you all the time, in everything, in light and in darkness, in stillness and in movement, in roaring wind and gentle breeze, always closer to you than you were to yourself."

These meditations and paintings on light and stillness can help us to become more aware that creation itself is a sacrament, a sign and an effective sign of God's presence, and that the world is, in Gerard Manley Hopkins' words, "charged with the grandeur of God."

OPPOSITE
A Flight of Crows

Painting and Prayer

In the myth of the fall of the soul to earth in Plato's Phaedrus, it is as if we journeyed once in a chariot atop the vault of the heavens, seeing there the ultimate reality and truth. Our soul then fell to earth where it "suffers from reminiscences." We experience glimpses, shadows or reflections of the "full vision of the perfect mysteries" we had seen above.[1]

Painting is one such form of "remembering." Painting is a way of looking, it is about the play of light on things. Painting requires a fresh way of looking at the world, a looking which presupposes "a deep subjective rapport with the object, an uncanny fusion with the object." It is about "being reminded of something never cognitively apprehended but existentially known, . . . before words existed," for example in our infancy. In adulthood, such experiences are often referred to as either aesthetic or sacred: "a feeling of being held by the object's spirit; . . . a caesura in time when the subject feels held in symmetry and solitude by the spirit of the object;"[2] an experience which belongs to no time, no place, beyond time and place, what Tillich described as the Eternal Now.[3]

In his lectures on Zen Buddhism, Suzuki contrasts a seventeenth-century Japanese haiku of Basho with a poem by Tennyson:

Yoku mireba   When I look carefully
Nazuna hana saku   I see the nazuna blooming
Kakine kana   by the hedge!

Flower in the crannied wall,
I pluck you out of the crannies;—
Hold you here, root and all, in my hand,
Little flower—but if I could understand
What you are, root and all, and all in all,
I should know what God and man is.

Suzuki observes that the Japanese word *kana* is untranslatable in English. It is often expressed in translation by an exclamation point, and refers to a kind of unutterable shock of recognition, an *ah!* or an *oh!* "Behold the lilies of the field," Jesus said. He didn't say, "Look at those lilies," but rather "behold," *kana*. Painting is about that attempt to capture the experience of *kana*. It is much less about the process described by Tennyson. In his attempt to understand the flower intellectually he plucks it, kills it, eradicating its beauty in the process.[4]

OPPOSITE

The Chapel of the Rock, St Beuno's, North Wales

View from the Silent Tent, Taizé, on a Rainy Afternoon

"By love he may be gotten and holden: by thought never," said the author of *The Cloud of Unknowing*.[5] Painting is about loving the object we see. We can really only paint what we love, or by infusing quite ordinary objects with the spirit of love within us. "Van Gogh painted his chair. He loved it, it was one of the few things he owned."[6]

The artist is familiar with the situation in which she has walked into a landscape to paint and is grasped by that shock of recognition, that *kana*: "Look at the light there. I must paint that." Painting is about an experience. "It comes out of the sweat and tears of trying to produce the unattainable. Art is a struggle between what we feel and what we produce."[7]

Some moments of aesthetic experience are also moments of prayer. They are moments of "reminiscence," when we glimpse something barely remembered, a shadow, a reflection of something never cognitively apprehended but existentially known. Socrates put it this way: "It has been poured into me, through my ears as into a vessel from some external source, though in my stupid fashion I have actually forgotten how, and from whom, I heard it."[8]

Painting is about this kind of looking. Christopher Bryant wrote of the French peasant who used to kneel for an hour every night with his eyes fixed on the tabernacle over the altar. When asked what he said during his nightly vigil he replied, "I don't say anything. I look at him and he looks at me."[9]

I found this poem on a piece of cardboard propped up on a chair in a chapel in a small country church in France. It expresses very powerfully what I believe painting can be about:

Quand on aime,
on voudrait parler sans cesse
de l'être qu'on aime

When one loves
one would wish to speak ceaselessly
of that being whom one loves,

ou, au moins,
le regarder sans cesse:
la prière n'est pas autre chose.

or, at least,
to look at him without ceasing.
Prayer is no other thing than this.[10]

Painting, at its best, is none other than looking at him whom we love without ceasing. In so doing we are remembering; we are held in symmetry and in solitude by the spirit of the object which is part of God's created world. We are experiencing something in time yet beyond time, we are one with him.

Maundy Thursday Vigil

Infinity

Why *does* the infinity come through how the light plays on something? We might begin by considering the *play* of light on things. The light changes. At least in England, it does. We tend not to have those long, uniformly sunny days that occur in North America. In countries where the sun blazes down all day, it is usually the slanting light of early morning or late afternoon that has the same effect on us, as the sun moves relatively quickly overhead in relation to the horizon.

> Sunlight slanting down a broad glade between two woodlands that drowsed in the summer heat. . . . A deep silence held it: the water slid without noise under the footboards, no note of bird broke the afternoon hush.[1]

The play of light on things is momentary and elusive. In the experience of "now" is contained the awareness that now is fleeting.

Through the experience of the passage of time from moment to moment comes the idea of that endless procession of moments into infinity, and out of the infinite procession of moments it is not far to thoughts of the eternal—"epiphanies of another order of reality."[2]

Light is fragile, temporal. Look at light and admire its beauty. Close your eyes and observe. That which you saw before is no more, and that you will see after is not yet.[3] The light we see now will never be exactly the same again because like time, it is flying:

> My old home
> Now but a night's lodging;
> Birds of passage.[4]

In a moment this particular light will be gone, its angle on objects will change. It is:

> . . . here a moment, then not here,
> like my belief in God.[5]

> I have seen the sun break through
> to illuminate a small field
> for a while, and gone my way
> and forgotten it. But that was the pearl
> of great price, the one field that had
> the treasure in it. I realize now
> that I must give all that I have
> to possess it. Life is not hurrying
>
> on to a receding future, nor hankering after
> an imagined past. It is the turning

Footbridge over Le Cousin

aside like Moses to the miracle
of the lit bush, to a brightness
that seemed as transitory as your youth
once, but is the eternity that awaits you.[6]

. . . A hill lights up
Suddenly; a field trembles
With colour and goes out
In its turn; in one day
You can witness the extent
Of the spectrum and grow rich
With looking. . . .[7]

To the dying person, the whole of existence is *now*:

We tend to forget that life can only be defined in the present tense, it *is, is, is*.
And it is *now, only*. The only thing you know *for sure* is the present tense. And
that *nowness* becomes so vivid to me that in a perverse sort of way, I'm almost
serene, I can celebrate life. Below my window in Ross, when I'm working in
Ross now at this season, the blossom is out in full. There's a plum tree. It looks
like apple blossom but it's white. And looking at it, instead of saying, "Oh
that's nice blossom," now, last week, looking at it through the window when
I'm writing, it is the whitest, frothiest, blossomiest blossom that there ever
could *be*, you know. . . [But] the *nowness* of everything is *absolutely wondrous*,
and if people could see that, there's no way of telling you, you have to experience it, the *glory* of it, the comfort of it, the reassurance. . . . The fact is that if
you see the present tense, *boy*, do you see it, and *boy*, can you celebrate it, you
know?[8]

As day breaks, so does the certainty of death which we keep from consciousness
most of the time in order to go about our daily round:

Waking at four to soundless dark, I stare.
In time the curtain-edges will grow light.
Till then I see what's really always there:
Unresting death, a whole day nearer now.[9]

High Windows

Yet against death, even Larkin had to set life:

> Rather than words comes the thought of high windows:
> The sun-comprehending glass,
> And beyond it, the deep blue air, that shows
> Nothing, and is nowhere, and is endless.[10]

The poet captures a sense of brilliant, transcendent light without once using the word. Perhaps painting and poetry are both attempts to put light on paper.[11] In painting, the image of light created by the artist's hand and eye at one moment in time is unique. Paradoxically, this uniqueness creates in the viewer a sense of time-lessness. The light flickering across a landscape, as when wind blows clouds over the moors, is like a cross-section through time, an intersection between the temporal (horizontal) and the eternal (vertical).

> Monet's paintings of the cathedral are about time. They depict the mad race of hours, minutes, seconds—through light. . . . Each painting is the immediate vision of an effect that took place instantaneously on the cathedral façade, in front of Monet's eyes. To catch the effect of a few minutes of a given hour, indicated by the position of the light on the wall, is one essential point of each painting of the cathedral. . . . It may not be sheer coincidence that almost every painting of the cathedral centres on the clock; a clock that, ironically a victim of the vicissitudes of time, eventually fell off the wall and is no longer visible. . . . Each painting is depicting the "right now," the hour that is marked on the clock—which, however, Monet chose to blur with paint. The clock reveals only a crust of colours. . . . Each painting is the truth of an instant, negated by the one before, and the one after.[12]

> They made the grey stone
> Blossom, setting it on a branch
> Of the mind; airy cathedrals
> Grew, trembling at the tip
> Of their breathing; delicate palaces
> Hung motionless in the gold,
> Unbelievable sunrise. . . .[13]

Clerestory, Ely Cathedral

Enlightenment

The light of the body is the eye.[1] The eye is the window of the soul.[2] May it please the Lord, light of all things, to illuminate me so that I can worthily deal with light.[3] If we look deeply into the world its freshness and beauty may be revealed to us in a new way: "The deep eye sees the shimmer on the stone."[4] Looking can become a "sacrament of the present moment"[5] or "the practice of the presence of God."[6] Gerard Manley Hopkins devised his own language for the uniqueness of the object before him, its individually distinctive form. He called it *inscape*, and the energy which kept it in being he called *instress*:[7]

> I do not think I have ever seen anything more beautiful than the bluebell I have been looking at. I know the beauty of our Lord by it.[8]

But the artist is not only an acute observer—a photograph can select a part of the world and place a frame around it. The painter is a participant as well as an observer. A painting is a whole creation.[9]

> Give beauty back,
> Beauty, beauty, beauty back to God. . . .[10]

There is the light of revelation, when something is suddenly made dazzlingly clear:

> . . .There have been times
> when, after long on my knees
> in a cold chancel, a stone has rolled
> from my mind, and I have looked
> in and seen the old questions lie
> folded and in a place
> by themselves, like the piled
> graveclothes of love's risen body.[11]

Abbaye de Sénanque

But enlightenment is not only clarity. "Light dissolves and merges things as much as it clarifies."[12]

There is the light of resurrection and new life—light "breaking over you like bread."[13] Among the paintings of Michel Ciry are many portraits of the disciples at Emmaus. Jesus is never shown, only his reflected light. Luke the Evangelist wrote of our risen Lord that when he was at table with two of the disciples, he took bread and blessed and broke it, and gave it to them, and their eyes were opened, and they recognized him.[14]

In the work of Michel Ciry there are two distinct domains, that of light and that of mystery. . . . That of light carries its own mystery. . . . One will at once understand that for Ciry the domain of light cannot be other than that of God. Therefore if there is mystery, it is from the outset because God is there. . . . Ciry, wrote François Mauriac, knows how to make a poor face such as we pass in the street radiant with divinity. . . . It is in the startled faces of the pilgrims at Emmaus that it appears most plainly to us, because they have seen Jesus, unseen by us, and having recognized him, their humility has been transfigured. All these faces reflect that of Jesus. God himself is beyond the canvas.[15]

> . . . Light pours on them
> and they lift their faces
> to be washed by it
> like children . . . .[16]

Snow Showers

Darkness

Sun smudge on the smoky water.[1]

Think of the contrast when the light goes, as behind a cloud: everything goes flat. Light creates in a landscape its third dimension, *transfiguring* ordinary things. Cast at an angle, light creates shadow on the ground. There is some music that is full of light and shade.[2] No consideration of light is complete without an account of darkness. In God's first act of creation, evening came and morning came, a second day.[3] God created "light in a dark frame," for light is known to exist only in relation to darkness.[4]

To "damage spiritually" means to put someone outside God's light, beyond the reach of God's sacraments, word, and forgiveness.

Thus far we have considered light more in classical than in romantic terms. Light in classical terms is balanced and rhythmic, like Vermeer's girl at a window. There is also disturbing, emotional, and violent light, as in El Greco's *View of Toledo* or Holman Hunt's *The Scapegoat*.[5]

O the mind, mind has mountains; cliffs of fall
Frightful, sheer, no-man-fathomed.[6]

If your eye is not sound, your whole body will be full of darkness. If then the light in you is darkness, how great is the darkness![7]

It is here that we enter our own inner wilderness:

. . . the backward half-look
Over the shoulder, towards the primitive terror.[8]

All kinds of nameless dread inhabit the yew tree's shade.[9]

This devastating sense of grey ashes in a burnt-out grate.[10]

I wake and feel the fell of dark, not day.
What hours, O what black hours we have spent
This night! what sights you, heart, saw; ways you went!
And more must, in yet longer light's delay.
With witness I speak this. But where I say
Hours I mean years, mean life.[11]

Apparition

Yet as a painter I am aware that "darks" are not black, they are full of various colours. Even in the darkest night—Christ lying in the tomb—there is the assurance of resurrection. That cold stillness is not unlike Easter Eve in the north of this country, but even in that landscape of late winter there is the promise of a morning.

> light in a hillside shed window
> calls a January day
> down.
>
> copses dying in salmon grey
> by a shadowless snowfield
> stand silent.
>
> a dusky bird
> comes searching for grain.[12]

An image of light in the darkness in a prayer for the Christmas season:

> While all things were in silence, and night was in the midst of her swift course,
> Your Almighty Word, O Lord, leaped down out of your royal throne.
> Alleluia.[13]

The darkness is no darkness with Thee, but the night is as clear as the day.[14]

Light will come to thee from longing.[15]

Rain over the Sea from Lindisfarne

Stillness and Listening

Attending to the play of light on things is a *poetic way of looking*. Paul Valéry wrote that walking is to dancing as prose is to poetry:

> Walking, like prose, always has a definite object. It is an act directed toward some object that we aim to reach. . . Dancing is quite different. . . . It is . . . a system of acts . . . whose end is in themselves. It goes nowhere.[1]

And yet, for that very reason, it can point beyond itself towards the infinite.

Compared to ordinary speech, poetry enters a quite different key and, as it were, a *quite different time*.[2]

> Our souls can, in the very heart of time, make for themselves sanctuaries impenetrable to duration, eternal in their inner selves, but transient with regard to nature; where they at last *are* what they know; where they desire what they are; where they feel themselves to be created by what they love, and render back to it light for light, and silence for silence. . . . They are like those sparkling calms, circumscribed by tempests, which shift from place to place on the seas. What are we during these abysses?[3]

> . . . After the kingfisher's wing
> Has answered light to light, and is silent, the light is still
> At the still point of the turning world.[4]

When asked where he has been, the poet can only say, "*there* we have been," he can only point towards it. The still point is no-time, no-place:

> . . . Except for the point, the still point,
> There would be no dance, and there is only the dance.
> I can only say, *there* we have been: but I cannot say where,
> And I cannot say, how long, for that is to place it in time.[5]

Ruined Cathedral, Ischia

Words can only approach it and, when we have finished speaking, there is this silence:

> I do not know which to prefer,
> The beauty of inflections
> Or the beauty of innuendoes,
> The blackbird whistling
> Or just after.[6]

There is a silence, a silence which is not an absence of sound but which is the object of a positive sensation more positive than that of sound. Noises, if there are any, only reach me after crossing the silence.[7]

Light listened when she sang.[8]

One of Michel Ciry's portraits is entitled *A l'écoute de Dieu*, listening for God.

> But the silence in the mind
> is when we live best, within
> listening distance of the silence
> we call God.[9]

When I say *an uncanny sense of light*, this is for me usually about a stillness and a listening, a silence in a landscape: "You can feel the air there."

> At dusk in spring the air is especially refractory
> A robin's voice is heard like crystal in the silence

> An answer
> And another call

> An answer
> And another call.

> The buds are heavy
> The trees are absolutely still
> You can feel the air now
> Out-of-time
> No-time.[10]

Not conscious
that you have been seeking
suddenly
you come upon it

the village in the Welsh hills
dust free
with no road out
but the one you came in by.

A bird chimes
from a green tree
the hour that is no hour
you know. . . .[11]

In the early light, the rock shadows on the snow are sharp; in the tension between light and dark is the power of the universe. This stillness to which all returns, this is reality, and soul and sanity have no more meaning here than a gust of snow; such transience and insignificance are exalting, terrifying, all at once, like the sudden discovery, in meditation, of one's own transparence.[12]

What do the clouds say?
These sweeps of light undo me.[13]

Under the thin smoke of winter,
the old temple is quiet.

After sundown,
all the visitors are gone.

On the west wind, three,
four chimes of the evening bell.

How can the old monk
concentrate on zazen?[14]

OPPOSITE

Larressingle

Evening Light

Light travelled over the wide field;
Stayed.
The weeds stopped swinging.
The mind moved, not alone,
Through the clear air, in the silence.[15]

It was hot and still. The breathless silence seemed unnatural, seemed, as I lay motionless in the tangled grass, like a bridge that reached straight back into the heart of some dim antiquity. . . . And a strange thing happened. For though there was no wind, a green leafy branch was snapped off from the tree above me, and fell to the ground at my hand. I drew my breath quickly; there was a drumming in my ears; I knew that the green woodland before me was going to split asunder, to swing back on either side like two great painted doors. . . . And then—then I hesitated, blundered, drew back, failed. The moment passed, was gone.[16]

For most of us, there is only the unattended
Moment, the moment in and out of time,
The distraction fit, lost in a shaft of sunlight.[17]

"Through a round hole, by this we climbed. . ."
Dante and Virgil emerge out of Hell into Purgatory

Unseen light

Alike pervaded by his eye
all parts of his dominion lie:
this world of ours and worlds unseen,
and thin the boundary between.[1]

Against all the evidence the world presents us, there is vastly more than what
we see. Underneath all that appals us, the world is God's, even so. . . . To see
something of the power and the glory and the holiness beneath what we
see . . . [2]

. . . one unseen light,
all, all is thine.[3]

Faith gives substance to our hopes
and convinces us of realities we do not see.[4]

We need someone to look at us intently to discern the faith in us[5]—*looking intently
and seeing beyond*, the man or woman of God who looks into our soul but who sees
with God's love and draws out what is in us of God. Looking intently and seeing
beyond is something I do when I paint. I don't paint only trees and skies. There is
something else there that I am painting.

Some ask the world
and are diminished
in the receiving
of it. You gave me

only this small pool
that the more I drink
from, the more overflows
me with sourceless light.[6]

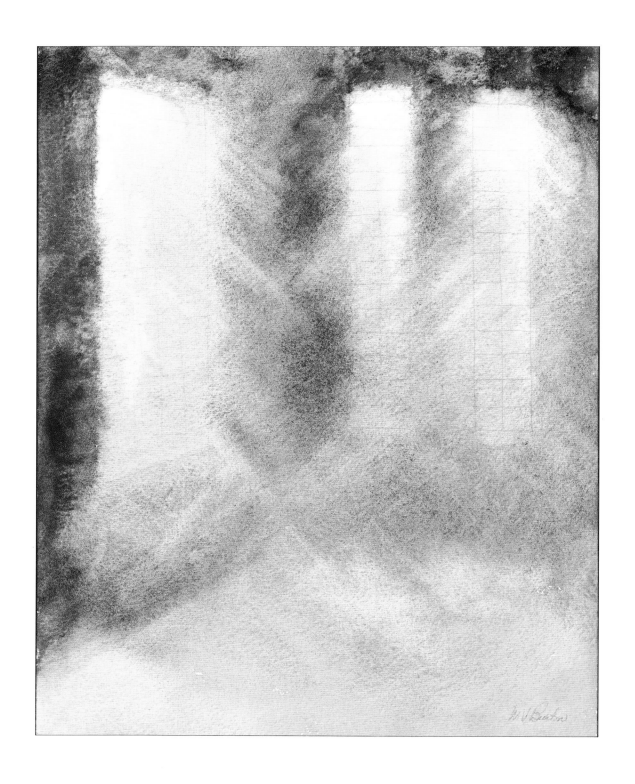

The Upper Room

Warmth, Gift, Love, Mercy

There is a cool northern light that clarifies,[1] but other kinds of light are warm and life-giving:

> He sends you rain from heaven and the crops in their seasons,
> and gives you food in plenty and keeps you in good heart.[2]

Light keeps us in good heart, too.

> When things of love and light happen, faith clings on to them for dear life,
> because that is what they are.[3]

> The breaking of the wave
> outside echoed the breaking
> of the bread in his hands.

> The crying of sea-gulls
> was the cry from the Cross:
> Lama Sabachthani. He lifted

> the chalice, that crystal in
> which love questioning is love
> blinded with excess of light.[4]

Let thy mercy lighten upon us.[5] Light personifies forgiveness. A correspondent in the contemporary press reviewing Monet's Cathedral series wrote:

> A mystic beauty suggesting the hours of forgiveness and of foregone memory at the threshold of impregnable church squares.[6]

The Annunciation

36

Presence

. . . Though you sit down
a thousand years, the echo
of the petals is inaudible
in the sunlight. . . .[1]

God is Light and those whom He makes worthy to see Him, see Him as Light;
those who receive Him receive Him as Light. For the light of His glory goes
before His face.[2]

the field tilts back,
nothing but light.[3]

Light in the abstract is more than descriptive.[4] It points to an unseen presence who
dwells in unapproachable light.[5]

The Greeks were aware of the dangers of looking directly in the face of Apollo—
you couldn't deal with the light. Apollo blinded those who pressed too close in
worship.[6]

Two weeks before leaving Rouen in 1893, Monet wrote to his wife Alice that
he was only then beginning to understand his subject. His letter included a
startling description of the way the light was changing with the advance of the
season: "Every day it is whiter; more and more it is blazing straight down. . . ."[7]

A guest spent the Jewish sabbath in the home of the young Baal Shem Tov
(Besht), and everyone slept in one room. At midnight the guest awoke and saw
a large fire burning on the stove. He cried out, thinking the house was on fire.
Then he saw a great light, fell back, and fainted. When he revived, the Besht
said to him, "You should not have looked at what is not permitted you."[8]

Of what is Torah composed? "Black fire on white fire." In this world we read
the letters, which are black, and ignore the background, which is white. In
reality we are living in a negative of the true print. . . . What we see as letters—the darkness—are only vessels, while the shining white spaces contain the
real meaning.[9]

Rock, and snow peaks all around, the sky, and great birds and black rivers—
what words are there to seize such ringing splendour? But again something
arises in this ringing that is not quite bearable, a poised terror, as in the dia-
mond ice that cracks the stone. The brain veers; the sun glints like a weapon.[10]

The Nativity

Shale loosens. Marl reaches into the field. Small birds pass over water. Spirit, come near. This is only the edge of whiteness.[11]

. . . I think he still comes
stealthily as of old,
invisible as a mutation,
an echo of what the light
said, when nobody
attended. . . .[12]

. . . There were times
when, bending close over a flower,
thinking to penetrate the transparence
of its expression, we lost our footing
and fell into a presence illimitable
as its absence, descending motionlessly
in space-time, not into darkness
but into the luminosity of his shadow.[13]

To lose oneself in the unfathomable, to plunge into the inexhaustible, to find peace in the incorruptible, . . . *to offer oneself to the fire and the transparency,* . . . and to give of one's deepest to that whose depth has no end.[14]

. . . No object can influence us by its essence without our being touched by the radiance of the focus of the universe. . . . It is precisely because he is the centre that he fills the whole sphere. . . . "The world is full of God."[15]

Like those translucent materials which a light within them can illuminate as a whole, the world appears to the Christian mystic bathed in an inward light which intensifies its relief, its structure and its depth.[16]

The delight of the divine *milieu* . . . is that it can assume an ever-increasing intensity around us. One could say that it is an atmosphere ever more luminous and ever more charged with God. It is in him and in him alone that the reckless vow of all love is realised: to lose oneself in what one loves, to sink oneself in it more and more.[17]

For with you is the well of life:
and in your light shall we see light.[18]

The Green Door

Pilgrimage

O send out thy light and thy truth, that they may lead me:
and bring me unto thy holy hill and to thy dwelling.[1]

By faith Abraham obeyed the call of God, and *set out not knowing where he
was going*, and came to the promised land.[2]

In the light standing you will see your salvation, you will see the Lord's
strength, you will feel the small rain, you will feel the fresh springs in the
power and light, your minds being kept low, for that which is out of the power
and light lifts up.[3]

Light is a symbol of pilgrimage, not just *Lead, kindly light*[4] and the processions of
Advent, Epiphany and Easter which we celebrate each year, but the entire life
pilgrimage which some tell us ends, as it began, in a tunnel of light.[5]

Help us to press toward that mark,
and, though our vision now is dark,
to live by what we see.
So, when we see thee face to face,
thy truth and light our dwelling-place
for evermore shall be.[6]

For now we see through a glass darkly; but then, face to face.[7]

Notes

Title
Adapted from 1 Peter 5:4 "... an unfading garland of glory.'" *The New English Bible* (The Bible Societies and Oxford and Cambridge University Presses, 1972).

Foreword
 1. Mary Burton, "Après-midi," (France, 1989).

Painting and Prayer
 1. Edith Hamilton and Huntington Cairns (eds.), *The Collected Dialogues of Plato* (Princeton, Princeton University Press, 1961), "Phaedrus," p. 496. "Suffers from reminiscences" is a paraphrase of J. Breuer and S. Freud, *Studies On Hysteria* [1893], *Standard Edition of the Complete Psychological Works of Sigmund Freud*, Volume II (London, The Hogarth Press, 1955), p. 7. The original reads "Hysterics suffer mainly from reminiscences."
 2. Christopher Bollas, *The Shadow of the Object: Psychoanalysis of the Unthought Known* (London, Free Association Books, 1987), pp. 16, 30-32.
 3. Paul Tillich, *The Eternal Now*, (New York, Scribners, 1956), pp. 122-132.
 4. D. T. Suzuki, "Lectures on Zen Buddhism" in D. T. Suzuki, E. Fromm and R. DeMartino, *Zen Buddhism and Psychoanalysis* (New York, Grove Press, 1960), pp. 1-3.
 5. Clifton Wolters, trans., *The Cloud of Unknowing* (Harmondsworth, Penguin Books, 1961), p. 60.
 6. Charles Bartlett, PPRWS, teaching at the Bankside Gallery in London, 1995.
 7. Charles Bartlett, *Ibid*.
 8. Plato, "Phaedrus," p. 483.
 9. Christopher Bryant, *The River Within: The Search for God in Depth* (London, Darton Longman & Todd, 1978), pp. 108-109.
10. Charles de Foucauld, source unknown, translated by Mary Burton.

Infinity
 1. Sir Arthur Quiller-Couch, *Memories and Opinions* (Cambridge, Cambridge University Press, 1944), p. 52. Quoted in Michael Paffard, *The Unattended Moment: Excerpts from Autobiographies with Hints and Guesses* (Naperville, Illinois, S.C.M. Press, 1976), p. 28.
 2. Paffard, *op. cit.*, p. 8.
 3. Leonardo da Vinci. In: A. D. Sertilanges, *The Thoughts of Leonardo Da Vinci* (Tours, Imprimerie Vincent, 1992), p. 4.
 4. Zen haiku, source unknown.
 5. R. S. Thomas, from "Moorland," in *Experimenting With An Amen* (London, Macmillan, 1986), p. 49.
 6. R. S. Thomas, "The Bright Field," from *Later Poems 1972-1982* (London, Macmillan, 1983), p. 81.
 7. R. S. Thomas, from "The Small Window," in *Selected Poems 1946-1968* (Newcastle-upon-Tyne, Bloodaxe Books, 1986), p. 113.
 8. Dennis Potter on Channel Four Television. *An Interview with Dennis Potter* (London, Channel 4 Television, 1994), an edited transcript of Melvyn Bragg's interview with Dennis Potter broadcast on 5 April 1994, p. 5. Potter died on 7 June 1994.
 9. Philip Larkin, from "Aubade," in *Collected Poems* (London, Faber and Faber, 1988), pp. 208-209.
10. Philip Larkin, from "High Windows," in *Collected Poems, op. cit.*, p. 165.
11. Michael Sadgrove, personal communication.

12. Joachim Pissarro, *Monet's Cathedral, Rouen 1892-1894* (London, Pavilion, 1990), pp. 22-23.

13. R. S. Thomas, from "Art History," in *Selected Poems 1946-1968, op. cit.*, p. 112.

Enlightenment

1. Matthew 6:22.

2. William Blake. From "The Everlasting Gospel," in *The Portable Blake* (New York, Viking Press, 1946), pp. 618-619. The original reads:
> This Life's dim Windows of the Soul
> Distorts the Heavens from Pole to Pole
> And leads you to Believe a Lie
> When you see with, not thro', the Eye

3. Leonardo da Vinci. In: A. D. Sertilanges, *The Thoughts of Leonardo Da Vinci, op. cit.*, p. 4.

4. Theodore Roethke, "Infirmity," in *The Far Field* (Garden City, New York, Doubleday, 1964); quoted in Nathan A. Scott, Jr., *The Wild Prayer of Longing: Poetry and the Sacred* (New Haven, Yale University Press, 1971), p. 86.

5. Brother Lawrence, *The Practice of the Presence of God*, trans. E. M. Blaiklock (London, Hodder & Stoughton, 1981).

6. Jean-Pierre de Caussade, *Self-Abandonment to Divine Providence*, trans. Algar Thorold (Glasgow, Collins, 1971).

7. W. H. Gardner, Introduction, *Poems and Prose of Gerard Manley Hopkins* (Harmondsworth, Penguin Books, 1953), p. xx.

8. Gerard Manley Hopkins, Journal, May 1870, in *Poems and Prose, op. cit.*, p. 122.

9. Charles Bartlett, teaching at the Bankside Gallery in London, 1995.

10. Hopkins, from "The Leaden Echo and the Golden Echo," in *Poems and Prose*, p. 52.

11. R. S. Thomas, from "The Answer," in *Later Poems 1972-1982, op. cit.*, p. 121.

12. Michael Sadgrove, personal communication.

13. R. S. Thomas, from "The Moor," in *Selected Poems 1946-1968, op. cit.*, p. 88. The original reads:
> ". . . while the air crumbled
> And broke on me generously as bread."

14. *Service of Word and Sacrament II* (Philadelphia, United Church Press, 1966), p. 20; The road to Emmaus: Luke 24:13-35.

15. *Michel Ciry* (Paris, La Bibliothèque des Arts, 1977), Introduction by Michel Droit, translated by Mary Burton, pp. 10-11.

16. R. S. Thomas, from "West Coast", in *Experimenting with an Amen, op. cit.*, p. 29.

Darkness

1. Archibald MacLeish, "Autumn," in *The Collected Poems of Archibald MacLeish* (Boston, Houghton Mifflin), p. 163.

2. B.B.C. Radio 3 commentator.

3. Genesis 1:8

4. Freema Gottlieb, *The Lamp of God: A Jewish Book of Light* (Northvale, New Jersey, Jason Aronson, 1989), pp. 6, 9, 10.

5. Michael Sadgrove, personal communication.

6. Gerard Manley Hopkins, from "No worst, there is none," *Poems and Prose of Gerard Manley Hopkins, op. cit.*, p. 61.

7. Matthew 6:23.

8. T. S. Eliot, from "The Dry Salvages, Four Quartets," in *Collected Poems 1909-1962* (New York, Harcourt, Brace & World), p. 195.

9. Michael Paffard, *The Unattended Moment, op. cit.*, p. 119, in a reference to the yew tree in T. S. Eliot's "Burnt Norton."

10. Virginia Woolf, *The Waves* (London, The Hogarth Press, 1931); quoted in Paffard, *The Unattended Moment*, p. 114.

11. Hopkins, from "I wake and feel the fell of dark, not day," *Poems and Prose*, p. 62.

12. Mary Burton, untitled poem, Vermont, 1975.

13. Adapted from Christmas Vespers, Western Rite. In: Colin Semper, *Intercessions at Worship* (London, Mowbray, 1992), p. 54. After Wisdom 18:14, 15:

> For while gentle silence enveloped all things,
> and night in its swift course was now half gone,
> thy all-powerful word leaped from heaven, from the royal throne.

14. Psalm 139:12

15. Quotation from a Sufi poet from Sind cited in Irina Tweedie, *The Chasm of Fire* (Shaftesbury, Element Books, 1979), p. 46.

Stillness and Listening

1. Paul Valéry, *The Art of Poetry*, trans. Denise Folliot (New York, Vintage Books, 1958), pp. 206-207.

2. *Ibid.*, p. 285.

3. Valéry, "Dance and the Soul," in *Dialogues*, trans. William McCausland Stewart (New York, Bollingen, 1956), p. 78.

4. T. S. Eliot, from "Four Quartets: Burnt Norton," in *Collected Poems 1909-1962, op. cit.*, p. 180.

5. *Ibid.*, p. 177.

6. Wallace Stevens, from "Thirteen Ways of Looking at a Blackbird," in *Poems* (New York, Random House, 1959), p. 12.

7. Simone Weil, "Spiritual Autobiography," in *Waiting on God* (London, Routledge and Kegan Paul, 1951), p. 24.

8. Theodore Roethke, from "Light Listened," in *The Far Field* (Garden City, New York, Doubleday, 1964); quoted in Nathan A. Scott, Jr., *The Wild Prayer of Longing, op. cit.*, p. 81.

9. R. S. Thomas, untitled, from *Counterpoint* (Newcastle-upon-Tyne, Bloodaxe Books, 1990), p. 50.

10. Mary Burton, from "Robin" (Chicago, 1971).

11. Thomas, from "Arrival," in *Later Poems 1972-1982, op. cit.*, p. 203.

12. Peter Matthiessen, *The Snow Leopard* (London, Chatto and Windus, 1979), p. 162.

13. Theodore Roethke, from "The Lost Son," in *Collected Poems* (London, Faber and Faber, 1968), pp. 53-54.

14. Ma Chih-yuan, "Evening Bells Near a Temple," in *Midnight Flute: Chinese Poems of Love and Longing*, trans. Sam Hamill (London, Shambhala, 1994), p. 128.

15. Roethke, from "The Lost Son," p. 55.

16. Forrest Reid, *Apostate* (London, Constable, 1946), p. 149; quoted in Michael Paffard, *The Unattended Moment, op. cit.*, p. 61.

17. Eliot, from "The Dry Salvages, Four Quartets," in *Collected Poems 1909-1962, op. cit.*, p. 199.

Unseen light

1. J. Conder, "The Lord is King," Hymn 107, *Hymns Ancient and Modern New Standard* (Bungay, Hymns Ancient and Modern Limited, p. 231).

2. Colin Semper, sermon in Westminster Abbey, Pentecost 19, October 1993; after Frederick Buechner's "Faith," in *A Room Called Remember* (San Francisco, Harper, 1984), pp. 13-23.

3. From an anthem by H. R. Bramley, "Great Lord of lords," music by Charles Wood.

4. Hebrews 11:1.

5. Acts 14:9.

6. R. S. Thomas, "Gift," in *Experimenting with an Amen, op. cit.*, p. 13.

Warmth, Gift, Love, Mercy

1. Michael Sadgrove, personal communication.

2. Acts 14:17.

3. Colin Semper, *Intercessions at Worship, op. cit.*, p. 74. After Frederick Buechner's "Faith."

4. R. S. Thomas, untitled, from *The Echoes Return Slow* (London, Macmillan, 1988), p. 69.

5. "Te Deum Laudamus," from *The Book of Common Prayer*.

6. Joachim Pissarro, *Monet's Cathedral, op. cit.*, p. 31.

Presence

1. R. S. Thomas, from "The Bank," in *Experimenting with an Amen, op. cit.*, p. 21.

2. Vladimir Lossky, quoting St Symeon the New Theologian, in *The Mystical Theology of the Eastern Church* (Cambridge, James Clarke, 1957), p. 218; quoted in Fraser Watts and Mark Williams, *The Psychology of Religious Knowing* (Cambridge, Cambridge University Press, 1988), p. 30.

3. Robert Pack, from "At this distance," in *Nothing but Light* (New Brunswick, New Jersey, Rutgers University Press, 1972), p. 23.

4. Michael Sadgrove, personal communication.

5. 1 Timothy 6:16.

6. Helen Palmer, *The Enneagram* (San Francisco, Harper, 1988), p. 45, quoting Ursula LeGuin, *The Left Hand of Darkness* (New York, Ace Books, 1969), Introduction.

7. Joachim Pissarro, *Monet's Cathedral, op. cit.*, p. 47.

8. *Shivhei ha-Besht*, trans. and ed. Dan Ben-Amos and Jerome R. Mintz (Bloomington, Indiana, Indiana University Press, 1970), p. 30; quoted in Freema Gottlieb, *The Lamp of God, op. cit.*, p. 164.

9. Gottlieb, *The Lamp of God*, p. 10.

10. Peter Matthiessen, *The Snow Leopard, op. cit.*, p. 208.

11. Theodore Roethke, from "The Shape of the Fire," in *Collected Poems, op. cit.*, p. 61.

12. Thomas, from "Coming," in *Experimenting with an Amen, op. cit.*, p. 5.

13. Thomas, from untitled, in *Counterpoint, op. cit.*, p. 48.

14. Teilhard de Chardin, *Le Milieu Divin: An Essay on the Interior Life* (London, Collins, 1957), p. 118.

15. *Ibid.*, pp. 101-102.

16. *Ibid.*, pp. 121-122.

17. *Ibid.*, p. 123.

18. Psalm 36:9.

Pilgrimage

1. Psalm 43:3.

2. Hebrews 11:8.

3. George Fox, *Journal* (Epistle to Friends), ed. John L. Nickalls (Cambridge, Cambridge University Press, 1952), pp. 183-4; quoted in Brenda C. Heales and Chris Cook, *Images and Silence* (London, Quaker Home Service), p. 24.

4. John Henry Newman, "Lead, kindly light," Hymn 215, *Hymns Ancient and Modern New Standard, op. cit.*, p. 485.

5. For recent research on "near-death experiences," see for example R. M. Moody, *Life After Life* (Atlanta, Georgia, Mockingbird Books, 1975) and Rachel Noam, *The View From Above* (Lakewood, New Jersey, C.I.S. Publishers, 1992).

6. George Caird, "Not far beyond the sea nor high," Hymn 401, *Hymns Ancient and Modern New Standard*, p. 885.

7. 1 Corinthians 13:12.

About the Paintings

The paintings are about what has been revealed to me through my right hand. The thoughts and associations expressed in the text have grown out of the paintings. None of them was painted in order to illustrate an idea. In that sense they are neither description nor illustration, but they have inspired much thought and further reflection and it is hoped that they may for the reader as well, hence the book.

Frontispiece. A Flight of Crows
Background shadows cast onto paper by late afternoon sunlight through new leaves. The crows appeared later. Cornwall, May 1997.

1. *The Chapel of The Rock, St Beuno's, North Wales*
From an Ignatian retreat on a very still afternoon, July 1994.

2. *View from the Silent Tent, Taizé, on a Rainy Afternoon*
From a silent retreat at the monastery of Taizé in Burgundy, August 1990.

3. *Maundy Thursday Vigil*
In the chapel at St Peter's Belsize Park, London, April 1995. Twelve candles, one guttering.
Photograph by P. J. Gates Photography Ltd.

4. *Footbridge over Le Cousin*
A sunny afternoon near Pontaubert, Burgundy, August 1992.
Photograph by P. J. Gates Photography Ltd.

5. *High Windows*
Clerestory, Westminster Abbey, late afternoon, March 1995. Named after Philip Larkin's poem by the same title.
Photograph by P. J. Gates Photography Ltd.

6. *Clerestory, Ely Cathedral*
In the nave on Easter Eve, March 1997.

7. *Abbaye de Sénanque*
A chapel of the abbey church in Provence, April 1990.

8. *Snow Showers*
Seen on a drive from York to Scarborough in March 1995.

9. *Apparition*
The angel "appeared" in the doorway whilst I was mopping up an excess of dark paint. Modelled loosely after The Chapel of The Rock, St Beuno's, North Wales, November 1994. Michael Sadgrove said of this painting, "The presence of the cross says there will be resolution, but the rest of the painting says it will be achieved at a cost."
Photography by P. J. Gates Photography Ltd.

10. *Rain over the Sea from Lindisfarne*
From a retreat at Holy Island, Northumberland, June 1994.

11. *Ruined Cathedral, Ischia*
In the ruins at Ischia, Bay of Naples, April 1989.

12. *Larressingle*
A still afternoon in a mediaeval fortified village in Gascony, late December 1990.

13. *Evening Light*
Pillars in Westminster Abbey appear as windows through which the evening light is shining. August 1996.

14. *"Through a round hole; by this we climbed. . ." Dante and Virgil emerge out of Hell into Purgatory*
An exercise on a watercolour painting course with Bob Kilvert at Weobley, Herefordshire, August 1994. Thanks to Alan Jones, Dean of Grace Cathedral, San Francisco, for naming the painting.

15. *The Upper Room*
Blazing light at the end of the day in an upper room. Inspired by an Ignatian prayer on John 20 led by Fr Gerard W. Hughes, S.J., February 1996.

16. *The Annunciation*
Another study of The Chapel of the Rock, St Beuno's. The angel is blazing light in the doorway, Mary is invisible on the bench. November 1994.

17. *The Nativity*
Blazing light from the stable door, November 1994.
Photograph by P. J. Gates Photography Ltd.

18. *The Green Door*
In the cloister of the Certosa di S. Giacomo, Capri, Bay of Naples, on an Easter retreat in 1988.

Acknowledgments

The author and publisher acknowledge with thanks permission to reproduce copyright material as listed below:

The first chapter, "Painting and Prayer," was published under the same title in a slightly different version in *Modern Churchman*, Vol. 33 part 2 (1991), pp. 27-9, and is reprinted with permission.

Macmillan General Books for excerpts from the poems "Moorland," "West Coast," "Gift," and "Coming" from *Experimenting With An Amen* by R. S. Thomas; "The Bright Field", "The Answer," and "Arrival" from *Later Poems 1972-1982* by R. S. Thomas; and "Untitled" from *The Echoes Return Slow* by R. S. Thomas.

Cambridge University Press for excerpts from *Memories and Opinions* by Sir Arthur Quiller-Couch; *The Phaedrus* by Plato; George Fox's *Journal*; and *The Mystical Theology of the Eastern Church* by James Clark.

Jason Aronson Inc. for excerpts from *The Lamp of God* by Freema Gottlieb. Reprinted by permission of the publisher, Jason Aronson, Inc., Northvale, NJ © 1989.

SCM Press Ltd. for excerpts from Michael Paffard's *The Unattended Moment*.

Excerpts from *Monet's Cathedral* produced by Breslich & Foss Ltd. and published by Pavilion Books.

Excerpt from *The River Within* by Christopher Bryant published and copyright 1983 by Darton, Longman & Todd Ltd. and used by permission of the publishers.

Excerpts from *The Snow Leopard* by Peter Matthiessen, first published in Great Britain by Chatto & Windus 1979. Paperback edition first published 1989 by Harvill. © Peter Matthiessen 1978. Reproduced by permission of The Harvill Press.

Dan Ben-Amos for an excerpt from *Shivhei ha-Besht*, translated and edited by Dan Ben-Amos and Jerome R. Mintz.